HEALING OF THE
FRACTURED SOUL

A WALK IN SUCH FREEDOM THAT YOU WILL NEVER FEAR BEING HURT AGAIN.

Dr. Steve Shamblin

OlivePress
צהר זית

Messianic & Christian Publisher

HEALING OF THE FRACTURED SOUL

A WALK IN SUCH FREEDOM THAT YOU WILL NEVER FEAR BEING HURT AGAIN.

Dr. Steve Shamblin

HEALING OF THE FRACTURED SOUL

Front cover photo copyright © 2012 by Mayovskyy Andrew at Shutterstock.com, all rights reserved, used by permission.
Back cover photo copyright © 2012 by Simon Gurney at Shutterstock.com, all rights reserved, used by permission.
Drawing on pp. 42,72, and 88 © 2012 by Bigbadvoo at Flickr.com, all rights reserved, used by permission.

Cover design by Miriam Remington with Olive Press

All Scriptures with references are taken from The Modern Language Bible, The New Berkeley Version in Modern English Revised Edition.* Copyright © 1945, 1959, 1969 by Hendrickson Publishers, Inc. New Testament section, Copyright © 1945 by Gerrit Verkuyl. Revised Edition Copyright © 1969 third printing by the Zondervan Publishing House. Assigned 1990 to Hendrickson Publishers, Inc.

*This version is no longer in print. It is very similar to the New International Version 1984.

Published by
Olive Press
Messianic and Christian Publisher
www.olivepresspublisher.org
olivepressbooks@gmail.com

Messianic & Christian Publisher

ISBN 978-0-9847111-9-2
1. Christian Ministry - Counseling & Recovery
2. Christian Ministry - Personal & Family Life
3. Self-Help : Personal Growth - Happiness

TABLE OF CONTENTS

Chapter Two: The Rejection Cycle 45

Chapter Three: The Performance Cycle 75

How God Brought All This To My Attention 91

DEDICATION

I would like to say how grateful I am to the Lord for bringing me my wife, Denise, and for His calling upon our lives. The time the Lord allowed us to have with Rev. Ken Wright and his wife, Shirley, was more precious than gold. We are forever grateful for their love, input, and mentoring into our lives. Also, Dr. Bruce and Barbara Thompson and Loren and Darlene Cunningham who were used of God in many ways over the years to pour into us of what God has deposited in them. We are very grateful for these relationships and many others. It would take up many pages to say thank you to everyone who deserves some recognition from us. As we grow older, we realize how incredibly valuable long and lasting relationships truly are.

A very special thanks to my wife who has stood with me all these years walking out the call of God. Her commitment is very much a part of my calling and the ministry. A very special thanks also to my daughter who has also walked with us in the call of God and this ministry. We are very blessed by God's gift to us in her and are very proud of her.

FORWARD

I have been involved in international ministry for over thirty years. One observation is clear. Many in the Body of Christ are hurting and wounded. As a result, they may spend a lifetime trying to understand and overcome what has happened to them. They may also live out their lives in bondage to the hurts and wounds which rob them from entering into all the Lord has planned and purposed for them. Our goal in putting together this book is for you, the reader, to be set free by God's Spirit from all bondage to hurts, wounds, and unhealthy life cycles.

Dr. Steve Shamblin

CHAPTER ONE:

WOUNDED SPIRIT

Chapter One

NO PROBLEM TOO LARGE

As we begin our journey into a place of emotional healing and freedom, let me say that I am asked to help people just like you all the time with a variety of problems. Don't ever let the enemy try and tell you that your problem is the worst, that nobody else has the problem you have or to the degree you have. The Lord is full of compassion and able to heal to the utmost. So be encouraged. Your situation is not too difficult for Him.

People ask me for help with struggles in various things, with varying degrees of severity: marriage, hatred, bitterness, offense, sexual sin, etc. By the grace of God, each one has been helped as they came to understand the Biblical reality of what a wounded spirit is and the impact it can have on a person's life. I remember one young lady standing up during one of my seminars and sharing that when she was a little girl, her sister told her that if she would only take her life it would be such a help to the whole family and would relieve the financial pressure they were under. That young lady spent her life in and out of mental wards, suffering under the pressure and guilt of what her sister had shared with her. She took on the blame and over time believed she had mental problems. After she shared, I explained to her how her sister's words had wounded her spirit at a very early age and that she really didn't have any mental disease. She just cried and cried and God healed her.

LADY IN SWITZERLAND

Another time I was speaking to a group of missionaries in Switzerland when a young lady stood up and said, "Could I share with you something nobody knows? When I was born my father wanted a son. He was so disappointed that he has never accepted me as his daughter and has introduced me as his son all of my life." She was deeply hurt, wounded and crying. We came around her and prayed healing for every hurt and wound caused by this situation and the Lord did a wonderful healing in her life.

BIBLICAL TRUTH

I would like to submit to you, in a very simple form, the Biblical concept for dealing with those who are hurting in spirit and may or may not know it. There is no Biblical evidence that Jesus ever sat down with anyone and had them go back into their memory bank. Nor is there any evidence that Jesus ever sat down with someone and had them pretend to go back into their mother's womb to repair a past hurt. The Bible speaks of only one concept which gives us insight into the hurts and wounds of our lives and it is found in Proverbs 18:14, "*A man's spirit will endure sickness, but a broken [wounded] spirit who can carry or bear?*"

Wounded Spirit

WOUNDED SPIRIT

From a Biblical viewpoint, when a person is "hurting" there is only one perspective, not various schools of thought from which to choose. What people are dealing with, without realizing it, is a wounded spirit.

Looking at Proverbs 18:14, we see the seriousness of a wounded spirit. The fact is the Lord did not create us to carry or bear, in any way, shape or form, a wounded spirit. So what we have is a vast majority of mankind, saved or not saved, trying to do something which God says we were not made to carry. God's people are trying to do exactly what the Lord said they are not capable of doing. They are trying to live out their lives carrying around wounds in their spirit, which are manifesting in various ways because we can't carry or bear them. Please understand, right or wrong, innocence or guilt does not change the reality and consequences of a wounded spirit.

NO RESPECTER OF PERSONS

A wounded spirit is no respecter of persons. In every illustration that I share with you, the people involved were "innocent". They did not encourage, deserve, or in any way help facilitate what happened to them. Sound familiar? Unfortunately their innocence makes no difference when it comes to the reality of a wounded spirit and how it can dominate and control their lives.

Are you ready to look at your life, with the help of the Holy Spirit, and determine your need for your wounded spirit? Are you ready to then learn how to ask the Lord to heal you and effect a permanent change in you by His spirit?

A FIRST BIBLICAL REASON FOR A WOUNDED SPIRIT

Read Proverbs 15:4. According to this verse, what is the first Biblical reason a person can have a wounded spirit? _____.

Words have a powerful impact on our emotions, personality, and life in general. The word "wound" in this verse literally means to be "shattered" like a windshield that is shattered by a rock but still holds together.

That is the power of words spoken into people's lives. Their spirit becomes shattered and they may not even know it. All they know is hurt, anger, frustration, disappointment, etc.

THE UNBORN

Think of how many babies still in the womb are hearing words like, "I don't love you", or "I never wanted you". Every word spoken goes right to their little spirits and they come out of the womb severely wounded. Then years later, when personality disorders show up, the secular world adds to the wounding by giving them a psychological label for the rest of their lives.

One time while I was ministering, a young lady stood up, sobbing, and said, "That is what I did to my child. I use to beat my stomach and say 'I hate you'."

TEENAGERS

How many young people are suffering under the damage of words spoken to them by moms and dads who themselves are hurting and have been all their lives? Now we see **bitterness, hatred**, and **resentment** dominating and ruining their lives as a result of words that were spoken. I'm not saying this excuses their bad choices and actions. I'm simply trying to help you see and understand a cause of the real problem.

SPIRITUAL SOURCE

Read John 6:63. Notice what Jesus says about words, *"The words I speak to you are spirit and life."* As Christians, we have no idea what a blessing it is to have a Father who, when He speaks to the child, speaks words of spirit and life. We need to understand that words emanate from a spiritual source. The words you speak, or that have been spoken to you, are either words of spirit and life or they are words of hurts and wounds which ultimately produce death not life.

Lest you think we are exaggerating the importance of words, take a look at Matthew 12:35-37. The reality is we are going to be judged by the words we have spoken. Let us understand the words that come out of our mouth do carry power. They will either produce spirit and life, as Jesus' words did, or hurt and wounds.

HELD CAPTIVE BY ONE WORD

I remember sharing this concept of a wounded spirit when I was in Japan. A young Japanese man stood up and said, "I see it now. All my life my father has called me dumb and stupid. I never did well in school and always looked at myself as a failure. Now I realize how I have been held captive by the words of my father all my life." As we prayed for this young man, I asked him to forgive his father, and then we asked the Lord to heal every hurt and wound in his spirit. He was never the same again.

How many young people are dropping out of school or barely hanging on, and it has nothing to do with IQ or ability? But they are living out the consequences of words spoken to them by authority figures. Then the wrong choices they have made further complicate the situation. Their potential is never realized. The enemy has robbed more young people than we will ever realize, and it does not have to be so. God can still redeem every one.

HATE "BILLY" CLUB

I remember a young man we will call "Billy" telling me of his high school days. Because he was somewhat different in appearance, the other students created a "hate Billy club". The words spoken so wounded his spirit that his personality and character were radically shaped by the hurt he could not get rid of. As I shared, he realized what had happened to him and asked for prayer. The first thing he did was ask the Lord for forgiveness for the anger, bitterness, and resentment he had held against others. Then we prayed and asked the Lord to heal every hurt and wound in his spirit. I have seen him many times since, and the freedom which came is now evident throughout his personality and character.

BABYSITTING

On another occasion when ministering this message, a lady stood up and began to weep openly. Obviously the Lord was dealing with an area of hurt in her life. Slowly, she began to share. "One night my parents went out and left me with a babysitter. While they were gone, the babysitter sexually molested me. When my parents got home, I told them, but my father did not believe me. Not only did he not believe me, but from that moment forth, he began calling me a slut." I encouraged her to pray forgiveness toward her dad and the one who molested her, and I then asked the Lord to come and heal every hurt and wound in her spirit. Soon the flow of tears turned to tears of joy as the Lord set her free.

NO JUSTIFICATION

The careless words of authority figures have caused many mental, emotional, and physical problems. The situation is further complicated by the resulting choices the person makes. Let me make it clear here and throughout this book: what has happened to you is never an excuse to justify your life style. That philosophy simply will not fly. In the examples just shared, and those yet to be shared, every person was "innocent" and did not deserve what happened to them. Having said that, make sure you understand that their innocence does not excuse them from the bad choices they made out of their hurts and wounds.

YOUR PART

Having read these examples, list below the three most common areas of the heart that must be dealt with before asking the Lord to heal you.

1. b_____

2. h_____

3. r_____

WORDS SPOKEN TO YOU

Now we want to spend some time focusing on words which have been spoken into your life. List below the words that immediately come to mind which you now realize have been a source of wounds in your spirit. Remember, we aren't worried about covering every word right now. You can follow through in the future with other words that may come to mind.

1. _____

2. _____

3. _____

4. _____

5. _____

6. _____

7 _____

8. _____

As you look at your list of words, follow through a bit more and list out the attitudes, personality traits, and character traits you have developed as a result of these hurts and wounds and the choices you have made.

1. _____
2. _____
3. _____
4. _____
5. _____
6. _____
7. _____
8. _____

The next step is to forgive those who have spoken these words. Perhaps you do not feel capable of doing this. Ask Jesus to help you through His love, which He extended to you when you didn't deserve it. List those to whom you are willing to extend forgiveness.

_____
_____
_____
_____
_____
_____
_____
_____

Now because you have been willing to forgive others, we are going to pray and ask Jesus to come and heal every hurt and wound in your spirit.

Lord, Jesus, I ask you to come and heal me from the consequences of every word of death, which has been spoken into my life. I thank you for healing me and setting me free from every hurt and every wound. I thank you for setting my personality and character free to grow now in you and in your words to me. Lord, with your help, I want to become all you desire me to be. Thank you for your healing and your wholeness to me, amen.

Feel free to write your own prayer here.

_____

_____

_____

_____

_____

_____

_____

_____

_____

_____

_____

_____

_____

_____

A SECOND BIBLICAL REASON FOR A WOUNDED SPIRIT

Read Proverbs 17:22. Now write a second reason for having a wounded spirit, _____.

Yes, this is what I call an event based problem which produces physical symptoms. Notice it says "bones drying up". This is a physical symptom of a wounded spirit problem. Literally, in the medical profession, the drying up of bones is called arthritis. Now don't misunderstand me, I'm not saying every person who has arthritis has it because they have a wounded spirit, but according to Proverbs, some do. This is an area where people are dealing with a physical symptom that is rooted in a wounded spirit.

ON HER DEATH BED

I was in Africa, traveling with Pastor Ken from New Zealand. He was asked to go and pray for a lady who was dying. Her body was overcome with severe arthritis. As this pastor came into her room, he began to wait on the Lord and as he did, the Lord spoke and told him that she was in this condition because of deep rooted bitterness and hatred towards her husband. Pastor Ken then shared this with the lady and told her if she would forgive her husband, the Lord would heal her. Out of her mouth came an explosion of hatred towards her husband and no desire at all to forgive him. Pastor Ken sadly told her he was sorry, but without her letting go of bitterness she would not be healed, and left the room. Friends, it is not worth the selling of your soul to bitterness, hatred, and resentment. Do not allow these emotions to dominate and control you and your life all of your days.

LADY IN THE PHILIPPINES

During a ministry time in the Philippines, a woman approached me and asked if I could help her. She said she was struggling with fear and basically was afraid of everything. She had been to doctors, psychologists, and psychiatrists. They had given her every pill available, but nothing had really cured the problem. I asked her to share about her life. Immediately, she said, "I hate my parents." I asked her why. She said as a little girl, whenever her parents wanted to go out, they would lock her in a closet and leave.

Again, we have an example of something being done to someone who was "innocent". She did nothing to deserve being locked in a closet, but her choice to hate her parents had only complicated the wounding. I explained this to her and asked if she was willing to forgive her parents, and she said yes.

I also explained that the root of her fear was coming from the wounding which occurred in her spirit as a little girl being locked in a closet, and that Jesus was able to heal every hurt and wound. We prayed. With the wound healed, there was no more fear.

What is the wound Jesus needs to unlock and heal for you? _____

_____

_____

_____

_____

_____

_____

_____

_____

_____

I was sharing this story in another meeting. Two women stood up, asking for prayer because growing up they had also been locked in a closet. As we prayed for them, the healing love of God wonderfully set them free.

So many of God's people are suffering from physical, mental, and emotional problems, which are rooted in a wounded spirit.

A THIRD BIBLICAL REASON FOR A WOUNDED SPIRIT

Read Proverbs 15:13. Write in the space another reason for a wounded spirit. _____.

A spirit of sorrow can consist of many things including: disappointment, broken promises, loneliness, and mistrust.

Have you ever noticed how people can become depressed simply because it is Christmas time? I promise you something happened to them around this major event. I once heard a man share during a meeting that when he was growing up, his family had been very poor and he was always disappointed during Christmas. After spending some time with him and praying through this wound of sorrow, he also realized that he was trying to compensate for his past by giving and giving to his own children, not always to their benefit.

BROKEN PROMISES

My dad was in the military, so he was gone a lot. I remember he would always promise to do something with me when he came home, but when he returned he was always busy. Then the time came when he would have to leave again without keeping his promise. Dad never did this intentionally, and my response was not his fault, but over the years, I developed a real lack of trust toward people. If you told me something and didn't do it, that was it. You only got one chance. By the time I was a teenager I was a mess, hurting and lonely; yet unwilling to really trust anyone, let alone authority figures. Sound familiar? I remember my uncle promising to take me fishing. The day came and it was absolutely pouring rain. Did that matter to me? No way. He had promised something and nothing else mattered. When he canceled, I went into a rage and I'm sure my parents thought I had gone over the edge. How many parents witness a reaction in their child which is really a consequence of a wound?

I heard recently that forty percent of children in America go to bed each night without knowing the love of a mom or dad expressed in a simple act of saying good-night. Might you be one of those forty percent or one of the moms or dads that meant to be there, but somehow it never happened? Can hurts this deep be repaired? Yes! Nothing is too hard for God to redeem!

In the spaces below, write down the names and events which have lead to a spirit of sorrow in your life. If you are the parent, name the child or children to whom you have intentionally or unintentionally wounded with sorrow.

1. _____

2. _____

3. _____

4. _____

5. _____

Ask the Lord to open up your heart and help you embrace His love. For it is through the embracing of His love we are able to reach out and trust again.

_____

_____

_____

_____

_____

_____

_____

THE DIFFERENCE BETWEEN FORGIVENESS AND
A WOUNDED SPIRIT

One other thought before we leave this area of sorrow has to do with abortion. Abortion severely wounds the spirit. I have had many women come up to me and share how they have "darkness in their heart" or "sadness" around their heart or a "cloud" that seems to hang over them. They share how they have begged God for forgiveness, but nothing has made the "sorrow" go away. Then they ask if there is any hope for them.

Let's take a worst case situation. A girl is not saved, gets pregnant, and has an abortion. Later she gets saved and asks the Lord to forgive her. (I might add here that there is equal responsibility on the male.) My question to you is, what does true repentance equal? Very simply, true repentance equals true forgiveness. The conclusion drawn by so many women is that because the sorrow doesn't leave their spirit, God must not be willing to forgive them. They assume it is their punishment and they will just have to learn to live with it. Not so! God is greater than our hurt.

Read I John 3:20. The fact is forgiveness isn't the problem. Why? Let me repeat it again. It's because true repentance equals true forgiveness. You don't have to twist God's arm to get forgiveness. The problem is not forgiveness. Through abortion, the spirit has been wounded and needs to be healed. I have seen many eyes begin to light up again with hope when they are told this. When they realize the problem is not forgiveness but a wounded spirit, we pray, and the joy and peace of God returns to their souls.

A CHRISTIAN LEADER

Upon hearing this message, a male Christian leader came up to me in tears and began to share. "I'm married with four wonderful children. Before I was married, I got my girlfriend pregnant, and it was me who drove her to the abortion clinic." Through the tears we began to pray for Jesus to come and heal every hurt and every wound in his spirit. Soon you could see the peace and joy of God's healing come over him. He had held that wound for so many years. It's never too late for Jesus to come and heal.

A FOURTH BIBLICAL REASON FOR A WOUNDED SPIRIT

Proverbs 6:32-33 gives us another reason for a wounded spirit. Fill in the space with your answer: _____.

I'm sure you are right, but I would like to add a few words to what you may have written down. As we read these verses in Proverbs 6, we realize it is talking about sexual sin, adultery, fornication, homosexual acts, lesbian acts, sex with animals, and abortion. I think you see the seriousness of this problem.

SEX IS REALLY A SPIRITUAL ACT

If we understand the realities of how we were made, it will help us to better understand the spiritual realities of sex. God is spirit and we are created in His image which means we are also, in reality, a spirit being. Our body is a temporary dwelling place of our spirit. Our body is made of dust and it shall return to dust. When a man and a woman come together in sex it is not, as the world would have us believe, just two bodies having sex. Rather, it is first and foremost, two spirits coming together and uniting through the act of sex.

Now, what I am about to tell you, I wish every high school and college student could hear. A girl about eighteen came into the clinic one day and said she was having trouble with suicidal thoughts. I asked her how long this had been going on and she said it started a couple of weeks ago! Now, this isn't rocket science. The next question is: What happened two weeks ago? After much probing, she confessed that she had sex with a guy. Not realizing that the man she had sex with was struggling with suicide, she had opened her spirit up through sex, to whatever was a part of his spirit, and afterwards began having similar thoughts of suicide. I know he had suicidal thoughts by deduction. After questioning her, there was nothing else in her life, that could be remotely pointed to, that could have caused thoughts of suicide. This is why most people who have multiple sex partners usually struggle with different types of depression, many times accompanied by suicidal thoughts.

Here is what I want you to understand. Because ***sex is a spiritual act***, when two people engage in sex, everything that may be a part of one person's spirit now has free access to the other person's spirit. That is why you can see severe personality changes and all sorts of other changes take place in a person from the consequences of sex outside of marriage.

A YOUNG MAN

A young man stood up in a meeting and began to cry. He was about six feet four inches with blond-streaked, black hair plastered with gel and pointed in different directions, and had earrings and chains hanging off of most everything. Slowly and quietly he began to share. "Nobody knows what I'm about to say. When I was a young boy, I was sexually molested. Would you please pray for me that the Lord would cleanse and heal me?" We gathered around him and prayed. The next time I saw him, he looked like a different person. The hair color had changed. Some of the earrings and chains were gone. But more profound was the inner change. He had a whole new countenance. What a precious work of healing the Lord had done.

A YOUNG WOMAN

A young woman stood up for prayer. She was crying uncontrollably. I told her not to worry and that she did not have to speak; we would go ahead and pray for her. She shook her head no. "I have to get this out," she said. With a whisper she began to share how a gang of girls sexually molested her at a young age. I moved in to pray but she stopped me and said that was not all. She said after that had happened, she vowed to sexually molest every girl she could, then dropped to the floor in a heap, sobbing. I came to her and began to pray. You could sense the Lord taking all the hurt and wounds away, washing her clean. After awhile, the peace of Jesus came over her and a smile of peace began to show through.

A YOUNG WOMAN IN CANADA

As I was sharing in Canada, a young woman in her late teens came up to me and said, "I've been listening to what you are saying about the wounded spirit. I would like for you to pray for me. What I am about to tell you, nobody knows. When I was fourteen, my uncle came home drunk one night and sexually molested me. I never told anyone. He has now come to live with us and I can't function. I can't sleep, eat, or do anything. Would you please pray?" We prayed and asked the Lord to heal every hurt and wound which had occurred in her spirit. She thanked me and went quietly away. The next night she came back to the meeting, came up to me and said, "I couldn't sleep at all last night." I told her we would pray again. She said, "No, that isn't necessary. I couldn't sleep because I was <u>so happy</u>!" She said for the first time in years, there was no more fear. Bless the Lord for He is good.

Notes_____

_____

_____

_____

_____

_____

_____

_____

_____

_____

_____

_____

_____

_____

A FIFTH BIBLICAL REASON FOR A WOUNDED SPIRIT

Read Proverbs 23:29-35. In the space below, write another Biblical reason for a wounded spirit _____.

Yes, as you read Proverbs 23, you realize that alcohol is one of the Biblical reasons for a wounded spirit. There are countless thousands of broken marriages, broken homes, and devastated children who, unless the grace of God intervenes, will continue to live out wounded lives caused by alcohol with the compounding problem of wrong choices.

What has been interesting to me is to see how some people in the worst of circumstances overcome because of not allowing bitterness to possess their heart. You think some would never have a chance for a normal life, and yet they do exceedingly well. Then there are those who live out their whole life blaming everything on their circumstances. What do you think makes the difference? _____.

Without a doubt, some of the people who have suffered life's worst situations have seemingly gone unscathed from the circumstances of their life because of their choice to forgive and to keep their heart in a right place before God. How about you? Are you going to live out your life in the bondage of wounds and unforgiveness? Never realizing who you really are and what God has for your life? How many years have already been wasted to bitterness and unforgiveness? You can choose **now** to extend forgiveness to those who hurt you and ask God to come and heal every hurt and every wound in your life. Remember, Jesus is our example and He extended forgiveness to a lost and dying world as He was hanging on a cross.

A SIXTH BIBLICAL REASON FOR A WOUNDED SPIRIT

The last Biblical reason for a wounded spirit I will share with you is found in Jeremiah 5:30-31. As you read this verse, what would you say is this cause for a wounded spirit? _____.

When I share this at meetings and ask how many have been hurt by "prophets" who have blown into town and given out all kinds of "words of God", it is amazing and sad to see how many of God's children raise their hands. May I share a few thoughts about this with you? First, it is not our responsibility to make a "prophecy" come true. If you are given a "word" from the Lord, my advice to you is to hold it lightly in your heart before the Lord and keep on obeying Him daily. If it is God, He will bring it to pass. Our responsibility is walking daily before Him; not to become preoccupied with a "word" letting it become the predominant focus of our life. Remember, Jesus said, "My words are spirit and life." If you have been given a "word" from God and it truly was from His Spirit, it will produce life.

The other thing that I look for when someone is giving a "word from God" is humility and a sense of the fear of God in their life. If I don't see any humility or fear of the Lord, then it is highly probable that I will take what is said with a grain of salt and forget it as quickly as it was given, in spite of all the loud noise and emotionalism wrapped up in the "word".

Let me say that this is not an exhaustive list but hopefully it will give you enough insight and understanding to deal honestly with the wounds of your life.

I would like to turn our focus now to Jesus and how He handled being hurt and wounded.

HOW JESUS HANDLED A WOUNDED SPIRIT

In Isaiah 53:4-6, we read some very familiar verses. Most of the time we read these verses and interpret them as speaking to us about how Jesus was bruised and wounded for our physical healing. I'm not taking away from that wonderful truth at all. What I would like to have you think about is that those verses do not just refer to the fact that Jesus was bruised and wounded for our physical healing, but that He was also bruised and wounded for the healing of our spirit.

Look at the ways Jesus was wounded for you:

1. He carried our sorrows.
2. He was afflicted.
3. He was bruised.
4. He was rejected.

What is very important for us to understand is this: ***Jesus was wounded in spirit for us; yet, He never functioned out of the hurt or wound***. As a result, the hurts and wounds were never able to become a part of forming His character!

When you and I do not handle hurts and wounds correctly, it usually creates damaging life cycles, which we will address shortly. Our personality, character, general state of mind, and happiness is all directly affected. Unwillingness to forgive simply produces barrenness of soul and spirit.

TWO WAYS JESUS HANDLED HURTS AND WOUNDS

1. FORGIVENESS

Luke 23:34 *"Father, forgive them, for they do not know what they are doing."* No one has ever, or will ever, suffer as unjustly as Jesus did. In the most extreme situation of unjust crucifixion and carrying the sins of the world, we see Jesus extend forgiveness.

The extending of forgiveness is crucial for your release, healing, and freedom. It is one of the ways Jesus handled the most extreme example of hurts and wounds. You can go for counseling until the rapture and be told any and everything and still not be healed. The example Jesus left for us is the one of extending forgiveness from the heart not just from the brain.

The extending of forgiveness is such a powerful principle bringing healing and wholeness to the individual. It is simple, but not always easy to do, because the enemy would like to see you remain in a place of bondage with unending talking and counseling. As I have said before, I see no need of trying to reinvent the wheel. Why not follow the example Jesus set for us in God's word?

Look at I Peter 2:21. *"To such experience you have been called; for Christ also suffered for you and left behind an example, that you might follow in His footsteps."* May I save you countless hours of counseling and who knows how much money? Jesus' example to us is **the extending of forgiveness**.

As I see it, the extending of forgiveness is not just for the other person involved, and obviously has nothing to do with them deserving it, but it has everything to do with you and your wholeness and future in God.

2. BECAME AN OFFERING

The second way Jesus handled hurts and wounds is found in Isaiah 53:10. *"Yet it was the Lord's will to bruise Him; He put Him to grief. When His soul shall constitute an offering for sin, He shall see His followers, He shall prolong His days, by His hand shall the Lord's will advance."*

What is the example Jesus has set before us here that we may follow in His footsteps? The answer is found in the words, *"His soul shall constitute an offering for sin."* Jesus became an "offering" to the will of the Father. This is the example of complete surrender to the will of God—becoming an "offering".

Now notice the blessings which are directly tied to the surrender and becoming an offering to the will of the Father: *"He shall prolong His days, by His hand shall the Lord's will advance."* What incredible blessings! His days are prolonged and God's will is advanced in His life.

The Bible speaks clearly that the Lord numbers our days. How God may choose to prolong any of our days is up to Him, but this blessing is linked to one who has become an offering to the will of the Father. Now notice the other blessing. It says that by the hand of God shall the will of the Father advance in the life of Jesus.

How many Christians are crying out in frustration for the Lord's will to advance in their life? They even become so frustrated that they finally give up; concluding God just does not love them. We need to put an end to this type of thinking and continual frustration. The example of Jesus to us in this passage is very clear. The advancement of the will of the Lord in your life or anyone else's life depends on our becoming an offering to the will of God. In other words, "Lord, may Thy will be done in my life".

Now the question of whether the Lord's will advances in <u>my</u> life becomes answered by <u>my</u> complete and absolute surrender to His will. Again, may I save you numerous hours of expense and counseling by asking you some very direct questions? Please take time and ponder each question prayerfully before you answer.

FIVE BASIC QUESTIONS CONCERNING THE ADVANCE OF THE LORD'S WILL IN YOUR LIFE:

1. How are you doing with all God has asked of you?
2. How are you doing with trusting Him?
3. How are you doing with complete and absolute surrender to His will?
4. What have you actually done in obedience to Him?
5. What have you failed to do which you know God has asked of you?

Picture an altar and be encouraged to come. Come to the altar and become an "offering" to His will and watch the will of the Father begin to advance in your life again.

KEY THOUGHT:

<u>YOU WLL LIVE OUT YOUR LIFE AS AN OFFERING TO THE HURTS AND WOUNDS OF THE PAST OR AS AN OFFERING TO THE WILL OF THE FATHER!</u>

I would like to share with you a few verses about the Lord as you go to Him for the healing of every hurt and wound of your life.

Isaiah 42:3 says, "*A bruised reed He shall not break, and a dimly burning wick He shall not quench.*" What a precious picture of our Savior who is so gentle in dealing with us. Compare His gentleness with the secular psychological systems of the world like electro-shock therapy and lobotomies.

Psalm 34:18,22. "*The Lord is close to the broken-hearted, and rescues those whose spirit is crushed.*" "*The Lord redeems the soul of His servants; all those taking refuge in Him shall go free.*" Are you ready to take complete refuge in Him? He is ready to set you free from every hurt and every wound of your life.

In Psalm 147:3 we find that "*It is He who heals the broken-hearted, and binds up all their wounds.*"

Now is the time to pray. We have held nothing back. I trust you are now in a place to come to Jesus who is the only one who can and will heal your wounded spirit.

Feel free to write your prayer to Jesus here.

_____

_____

_____

_____

_____

_____

_____

_____

_____

_____

_____

_____

REVIEW

Let's do some reviewing. What are the six Biblical reasons for a wounded spirit?

1. _____

2. _____

3. _____

4. _____

5. _____

6. _____

Which of these have affected you the most?

_____

_____

Write down your story before the Lord in preparation of giving it all to Him.

_____

_____

_____

_____

_____

_____

_____

_____
_____
_____
_____
_____
_____
_____
_____
_____
_____
_____
_____
_____
_____(Continue on pages 42-44, if needed.)

Write down the choices you have made compounding the hurts and wounds you received.

_____
_____
_____
_____
_____
_____
_____
_____
_____(Continue on pages 42-44, if needed.)

We can all struggle with forgiving someone. Yet, as we have seen, forgiveness is key to your healing and freedom. Meditate on Jesus and what He did to extend forgiveness to you on the cross. When you are able, before the Lord, list all the names of those you know He wants you to extend forgiveness to and pray for, extending forgiveness to each one.

_____

_____

_____

_____

_____

_____

_____

_____

Now that you have extended forgiveness would you like for someone to pray with you for the healing of every hurt and wound in your spirit? If there is no one to pray with, Jesus is with you and you can pray everything through with Him.

After praying I would encourage you to write down the new choices and directions you believe God is encouraging you to make.

_____

_____

_____

_____

_____

_____

_____

_____

_____

_____

_____

_____

_____

_____

_____

_____

_____

_____

_____

_____

_____(Continue on pages 42-44, if needed.)

How many of your friends need to hear and do what you have done? List them here as prayer projects to see them healed and set free.

_____

_____

_____

_____

_____

_____

_____

_____

_____

Feel free to write and/or doodle on these pages as you continue your soul searching and listening to the Lord.

CHAPTER TWO:

THE REJECTION

CYCLE

Chapter Two

TWO MAJOR CYCLES

There are two major life cycles, which develop as a result of not handling the hurts and wounds of our life correctly. One life cycle is "Rejection" and the other is "Performance". In this chapter we are going to look at the life cycle of "Rejection". The rejection cycle brings issues like self-worth, self-esteem, and identity into play.

SELF ESTEEM—SELF WORTH—IDENTITY

So many people of all ages and cultures struggle with self-esteem, self worth, and identity. Many struggle for their entire lives and sad to say, demonstrate to their children a life of insecurities. In searching for a way to help, I began to look at the life of Jesus, which led me to ask a basic question, "Why didn't Jesus have a problem with self-esteem, self-worth, and identity?" Of all the people who should have had a problem with any of these, it was Jesus. Yet His character never suffered the consequences of rejection.

Now the question becomes, "Lord, how did you do that? How did you go through all the hurt and rejection of your life, carrying sins of the world and not falling prey to self-esteem, self worth, and identity problems?"

DON'T RE-INVENT THE WHEEL

If we can figure out how Jesus was able to walk through the hurts and rejections of His life, then all we have to do is follow His example. If we can discover His "secrets" and apply them to our lives, then we don't have to re-invent the wheel. We don't have to chase after all manner of Christian and secular counseling with an unending number of hoops to jump through. This will be our goal as you walk through this workbook. We will seek to understand how Jesus went through all the rejection of His life without falling prey to problems of self-esteem, self-worth, and identity and then you will be able to apply the same principles to your life.

LET'S BEGIN—THREE BASIC LIFE QUESTIONS

There is a lot of turmoil in people's lives because they don't know the answer to what I call "three basic life questions". I draw these questions from the Gospel of John where the Scribes and Pharisees were trying to figure out the identity of Christ.

The first question they asked the Lord was, "Tell us who you are." Jesus answered and said, "I am the way, the truth, and the life." Notice what Jesus didn't say. He didn't say, "I am a carpenter." That was something He did, not who He was. Now let's ask ourselves the question, "Who am I?" What would you say? Most people would answer in the arena of what they do. They might say, I am a student, a doctor, a lawyer, an artist, or an athlete. What I want you to realize is that you are not the sum total of what you do.

Let's look again at the question, "Who am I?" We will give you the answer, but let's look for a moment at the input that you have been given from the culture around you. So who does the world say you are? For the most part, the world without Christ is coming from a platform of secular humanism. Basically, it says you are your own god. This is the message of the world that we have heard since we started school or before that.

What about your parents and your culture? Both of these are sources of input to the question. What have they been telling you since you were born?

_____

_____

_____

What about the church? Who has the church been saying you are, or have they been silent and left you to figure this out by yourself?

_____

_____

_____

Let me share a thought with you. Of all the people on the face of the earth, Christians are supposed to know who they are. It is imperative. How are we as Christians to go into all the world and preach the Gospel, helping others understand who they are and who God created them to be, when we don't even know who we are ourselves? That, in a nutshell, is one good reason why the job of world evangelism isn't getting done.

Let's examine this. How would you answer the question "who am I?"

_____

_____

_____

_____

_____

_____

_____

_____

Now, write down how you may have been influenced, good or bad, by your parents, culture, and the church.

_____

_____

_____

_____

_____

_____

_____

_____

_____

The second question the Scribes and Pharisees asked Jesus was , "Where did you come from?" Jesus' answer was simple yet complete. He said, "I have come from My Father." Again, they did not like His answer. The answer Jesus gave is very significant because it gives insight into why He did not suffer with identity problems. He knew where He came from and thus His identity was tied to the source of His origin. So let's ask the question, "Where did you come from?" How would you answer? Most would say, "I came from a mom and a dad." That is true, but there is more to it, which we will explain shortly. What about the world? Where does secular humanism say you came from? "From monkeys" or "from evolution" is the world's education system answer. The fact is, if you believe in evolution, I guess you should have a problem with self worth, self-esteem and identity. Fortunately, we can say like Jesus, we have come from a heavenly Father and this is key to healthy self-worth, self-esteem, and identity.

Take a moment and think about this question. We have all come from a mom and dad and maybe we just forgot about God creating us. Write down the influences you have drawn from your mom and dad—the influences that have helped form your identity, good or bad, of your family roots.

_____

_____

_____

_____

_____

_____

The last question which the Scribes and Pharisees asked the Lord was, "Tell us where you are going?" Jesus answered, "I am going home to be with the Father." This forms our third basic life question, "Where am I going?" For all those who know Jesus as Lord and Savior, we are also going home to be with the Father and live with Him forever throughout all eternity.

Being able to answer these simple basic life questions brought tremendous security to the life of Jesus.

1. Who are you?
2. Where did you come from?
3. Where are you going?

What I would like to do now is focus in on the significance of the first two questions. As we focus on the realities of who we really are, and what it means for us to be able to say we have come from our heavenly Father, we will discover the significance of the first two questions.

LET'S LOOK AT WHO GOD SAYS YOU ARE

Psalms 139:13-16 *"Thou didst possess my inward parts and didst weave me in my mother's womb. I praise Thee because I have been fearfully and wonderfully made; marvelous is Thy workmanship, as my soul is well aware. My bones were not hidden from Thee when I was made in secrecy and intricately fashioned in utter seclusion. Thine eyes beheld my unformed substance."*

One of the first principles of truth we can draw from this portion of scripture is, **no one's birth on the face of the earth was a mistake or chance!** God made you and the fact of the matter is, He is not intimidated by the circumstances of your birth. Nor is He intimidated by who your mom or dad is or was. Your mom or dad could have been the worst sinner on earth, but God still chose to create you. Why? Might it just be that God figured He was God and there isn't anything you and He could not overcome? His purpose in creating you was to see you fulfilled in His will and destiny for all eternity. Nothing in the circumstances surrounding your birth, including the condition or the parents you came from, intimidated or discouraged God in the least.

Now you have a choice to make, you can no longer justify your lifestyle by blaming your mom and dad, or the circumstances of your birth. You are now faced with the reality of taking accountability and responsibility for your life, your actions, and your choices.

I realize some people have had a very sad and difficult set of circumstances surrounding their birth, but everything I have said is true and still applies. Think about your birth circumstances and write down the areas you believe were a negative influence upon you at an early age.

_____

_____

_____

_____

_____

_____

Another principle of truth has to do with the emphasis on "inward parts". Now let me ask you a question. If we have "inward" parts, what else do we have? Obviously we also have "outward" parts. Our inward parts refer to the spirit and soul—our mind, will, and emotions. The outward parts refer to the body.

In gaining understanding of who we really are, we need to emphasize what the Lord emphasizes. He emphasizes the inward parts or the spirit and soul of man. Why would the Lord emphasize these? Because the spirit and soul are the eternal realities of who we really are.

What is really amazing is that the Lord doesn't even mention the outward parts. When you think about it, why should He? Where did the outward parts, our body, come from? As we read in Genesis 2:7, God formed our body from the dust of the ground. When we die, the body shall return to dust. Is it any wonder that the Lord puts no emphasis on the outward parts? The truth is, that is not who we are. What the Bible does say in Genesis 1:26 is this: We are created in the image of God. The inward parts refer to spirit and soul. These are the eternal qualities of man and the realities of who we really are.

Remember: you are a living soul and a living spirit made in the image of God. It is the spirit and soul which shall live forever; either with the Lord in heaven, or separated from Him in Hell.

YOU ARE A LIVING SOUL AND A LIVING SPIRIT

The Bible speaks of the devil roaming around seeking to devour the souls of man, not the bodies of man. In Galatians 2:6 it says, *"The Lord does not even regard human appearance."*

Herein lies one of the major problems in the area of self-worth, self-esteem, and identity. Since the day we discovered ourselves in the mirror, we began to draw our self-worth, self-esteem, and identity from our "outward" appearance. This has been reinforced by culture and society on a daily basis.

Let's try a little experiment. I would like for you to get alone with God and go over yourself from head to foot. As you go over yourself, be honest and talk things through with the Lord. How do you like your hair, your face, your size, and so forth? Remember the devil is a liar. He will try to convince you that God somehow made a mistake when He made you. The devil will try to convince you to never trust God in any area of your life. How could you trust God with the selection of a mate or your future or any area if He made a mistake with you? That is the snare.

TRUE BEAUTY

As we all are aware, the world's definition of beauty is completely focused on the body or outward parts.

Let's take a moment and redefine "beauty". Who is a beautiful person in the sight of God? It is the person who is showing forth the character of Christ through his or her life.

What about the handicapped person who is missing a hand or leg? Let me ask you something, is his or her spirit missing a part? No. That is why there are people, you may even know some, who are "handicapped" yet show forth the character of Christ more than a person who the world would say is whole and beautiful.

What a radical definition of beauty. Guess what. It is God's definition of beauty that will count in the end.

It may be helpful here to write down how you have been influenced and snared under the world's definition of beauty as you grew up.

_____

_____

_____

_____

_____

_____

_____

_____

_____

So where does our worth, value, and significance come from?

It comes from two truth sources which you have probably known since you were saved.

The first truth, which gives us worth, is that **we were created in the image of God.** The second truth is, **Jesus bought us with His blood.** We didn't do anything to earn or deserve either of these. But the reality of these two truths is what gives us worth, value, significance, and the foundation of identity. The problem is, most of our knowing is intellectual. What we must do is get our knowledge from the brain to the heart. We just have to learn to apply these truths to the depths of our heart, and it will bring emotional stability.

MARVELOUS CONCLUSION

So…if what I am saying is true, we can draw a significant conclusion. **God is to be our first and only true source of identity!** Obviously, a person can have many "sources" of identity, but when it comes to understanding our worth, esteem, and identity, we must have a clear perspective on the sources with which we are identifying.

Notes_____

_____

_____

_____

_____

_____

_____

_____

_____

_____

_____

BEFORE AND AFTER

As an illustration, let me share a few of my former sources of identity. When I was eighteen, the number one source of identity in my life, without question, was sports. I ate, drank, and slept sports. I also identified with things like TV, music (none of which was any good), and movies. Yes, I went to church sometimes and I believed in God. Now it doesn't take a genius to look at my list and draw a conclusion that this person has some problems, and I did. My major problem was that God was not my number one source of identity; thus, everything else in my life was out of kilter. This meant that my worth, esteem, and self-image were warped which produced the accompanying emotional instabilities.

What am I identifying my life with currently? For me now, it is God. Unless I am fooling myself, God is my number one source of identity. Next is my family. Then would come my ministry or work. After that are other things like sports, music, and movies. Friends, this isn't rocket science. If God is not your number one source of identity, then you have problems. The answer is to get God into the number one position of your life no matter what it takes.

For the first time in your life, you are on the road to discovering who you really are and where your worth, esteem, and self-image really come from. In this light, let's ask ourselves a question. What are you identifying yourself with? Let's do a before and after. Start with when you were young. What were the areas in your life that you identified with? Make a list from the most significant to the least significant.

Areas I identified with before Christ:

1. _____

   _____

2. _____

   _____

3. _____

   _____

4._____

_____

5._____

_____

6._____

_____

7._____

_____

Areas I identify with now:

1. _____

_____

2._____

_____

3._____

_____

4._____

_____

5._____

_____

6._____

_____

7._____

_____

YOUNG MAN WITH A DOG

I remember a young man coming into the clinic for counseling and he had a dog with him. After several minutes of silence he said, "This dog is the only one I can trust." As I waited, I felt the Lord say that he was identifying with his problems (not that they were insignificant) to such an extent that he was now seeing himself in light of his problems. In other words, this young man's number one source of identity was his problems. That was how he saw himself—one big mess of problems.

How do you see your mom or dad? Are they one big mess of problems? Maybe their life is full of problems, but is that who they really are? Do you delegate your love to them in accordance with the amount of problems they have?

What does the Lord see when He sees you? Does He see your problems? When the Lord looks at us, He sees someone who is made in the image of God and someone who is bought with the blood of Jesus. Yes, He sees your problems, but there is a major difference. Jesus does not delegate His love to us in accordance with the problems He sees in our life! Hallelujah! He loves us in spite of our problems!

How have you handled the problems of your mom or dad or others in your life? How did you answer the question just asked? Have you limited your love to them and justified doing so because of their problems? Many of us do. Then we have the nerve to turn around and thank God, (as we just did in the last paragraph) for loving us "in spite of our problems". There is a word that describes this, hypocrisy. Might we need to examine this issue before the Lord and repent for delegating our love to others (be it a mom or dad, or anyone) in accordance with the problems we see in their lives?

In Romans 12:2, Jesus said, *"And do not conform to the present world system, but be transformed by the renewing of your mind."* Here Jesus is warning us not to identify with the things of the world. If we do identify with the things of the world, two things will happen:

1. We will lose our true identity.
2. The world will overwhelm us.

If we learn to identify with Jesus as our first source, then we will discover our true identity.

How have you conformed to this present world system and thus been led into problems with your identity?

_____

_____

_____

_____

_____

_____

_____

_____

_____

_____

_____

_____

_____

_____

_____

_____

_____

_____

_____

_____

_____

_____

LET'S LOOK AT A KEY PROBLEM TO A HEALTHY SELF IMAGE

In Genesis 1:26, God said, *"Let us make man after our image, after our likeness."* We see from this verse that we were created out of an everlasting, unconditional love relationship. It is out of this love relationship that we receive our love, our acceptance, and our security. Just one problem, most of us are not looking to God to meet these areas of need in our lives. We are looking in all the wrong places.

Take Adam for example. God made him the same way. Adam was to draw his love, acceptance, and security from God's love. Again, there was just one little problem. Adam sinned, which is a rejection of God's love. So let's pick up the story in Genesis 3:8-10. *"In the cool of the day they heard the sound of the Lord God taking a walk in the garden and the man and his wife hid themselves among the trees of the garden from the presence of the Lord God. Then the Lord God called out to the man; He said to him: Where are you? He said, "I heard Thy sound in the garden and I was afraid because I am naked; so I hid myself."*

This is the first time we see fear mentioned in the Bible, and it is directly related to the potential of rejection. We need to realize the potential risk rejection carries with it. For Adam, being rejected by God, his authority figure, also meant losing his source of love, acceptance, and security. I don't think Adam realized all this as we see by his conversation with God.

Now God never asks a stupid question. Notice the question He asked Adam. "Where are you?" What do you think God was after? Do you think God was trying to figure out which tree Adam was hiding behind? I don't think so. I think God was trying to get Adam to realize something very significant concerning his relationship with God.

Remember God has created us for an everlasting love relationship. All our love, acceptance, and security are to come from this relationship. By Adam's disobedience, he put all this at risk.

Now the question, "Adam, where are you?" From where are you going to draw your love, acceptance, and security, now that you have sinned? By your sin you have rejected receiving it from God.

Isn't it interesting that here we see the first instance of fear and rejection in the Bible? Adam rejects God by disobedience and sin; and yet, it is Adam that winds up with a problem of fear and rejection. How true this is for you and me. By our sin and disobedience, we reject God; and then, we wind up with fear and rejection problems. Why? Because in rejecting God, we never realized that we were also cutting off our only source of true love, acceptance, and security.

Remember, God created us for an everlasting, unconditional love relationship. It is out of this relationship that we find the love, acceptance, and security our heart so desperately longs for. Getting this understanding from our brain to our heart, and from the intellect to the depth of our emotions is the challenge. The consequences of not walking in the freedom of this love relationship with the Lord can produce years of walking in a rejection cycle with the accompanying problems of self-worth, self-esteem, and a multitude of identity problems.

Notes_____

_____

_____

_____

_____

_____

_____

_____

_____

_____

_____

_____

_____

_____

_____

REJECTION CYCLE

Let me try and walk you through this rejection cycle. Understand, the life I paint may well resemble yours, but it also resembles the life of people around the world from every background and culture.

Rejection can begin as early as conception. The spirit of a child can receive rejection from mom or dad. An example of this is unwanted pregnancies. As I shared earlier, I remember giving a seminar on this and a lady stood up and began to weep. She then uttered these words, "I used to beat my stomach and say how much I hated the child within me." We came around her, prayed for her, and the Lord set her free; but think about the child. Before he or she even came into this world, he or she was already suffering under the consequences of rejection. This can affect the character, personality and emotional makeup of the child. Remember every child is looking for love, acceptance, and security. Why? Because that is how God made us. So, when a child comes out of the womb, who is he or she naturally going to look to for these things? Yes, mom and dad.

As any child begins to grow up and look to mom and dad for his or her love, acceptance, security, hurts, and wounds are inevitable. Moms and dads are not perfect. So, in this critical area, if the child is not getting what his or her heart is crying out for from his or her own parents, he or she will begin to look to other sources such as teachers, pastors, and others to meet this cry. As the child continues to grow, he or she will simply continue to look for love, acceptance, and security from one authority figure to another. Keep in mind that neither the child nor the authority figures know this cycle is going on. The child is not thinking this through.

So we see that early in life the child begins to experience hurts and wounds from authority figures. Yet, he or she unknowingly continues to look to authority figures for love, acceptance, and security. Let me ask a question. Have you ever had a problem with authority figures in your life? I have never failed to get a one hundred percent response when I ask this question. Why is that? The answer becomes simple when we understand the realities of how God made us. The reason we have problems with authority figures is because we are unconsciously looking to them and longing for their love, acceptance, and security.

This brings up another question. How about God? He is the "big" authority figure. It is no wonder that many struggle with the same insecurities toward God as they do with other authorities in their life. There is just one difference. God is the one to whom we are supposed to be looking for love, acceptance, and security. Not looking to God causes the cycle to continue.

FORMS OF COVER UP

As the child begins to grow into the teenage years, it is common for fears and insecurities to develop. Most teenagers are not secure enough to go around admitting they have fears and insecurities. Not knowing what is really going on in their lives or how to handle the fears and insecurities, they begin to develop forms of cover up.

These forms of cover up tend to take two basic paths. One path of cover up is through **withdrawal.** The other path is an **outward form of cover up.** What I want you to understand is that a person caught in this rejection cycle will tend to swing, like a pendulum, back and forth between these two forms of cover up. It all depends upon the setting or situation with which they are confronted with. Take my life, for example. Let's say I am in high school or college and asked by friends to go to a party. Parties were a threatening setting for me, although I didn't understand why. When asked to go to a party I would come up with an excuse—something like, "I have to study" or "I have to help my parents" or anything that would get me out of that environment where I was not secure and had a potential for failure. So, I would swing into my withdrawal form of cover up. We go into a withdrawal mode whenever we are confronted with a situation that is a threat to our receiving love, acceptance, and security.

On the other hand, if my friends came and asked me to play a sport with them, instantly I was dressed and out the door waiting on them saying, "Hurry up!" People mistake this outward form of cover up as security, but it is anything but security. It is simply that each of us has areas where we have found levels of love, acceptance, and security and we swing to that form of cover up. People look at us sports players and think that we are so secure. Nothing could be farther from the truth. We are just functioning in our outward form of cover up. Other forms could be humor, reading, art, music, computers, eating—the list is endless.

Remember, you will swing between your withdrawal form of cover-up and your outward form until you recognize the cycle you are caught in and ask the Lord to set you free. In reality, freedom from this rejection cycle is not just for you. It's important for your family and children that the cycle be broken and not reproduced in them.

Write down the situations that you would withdraw from throughout your life.

_____

_____

_____

_____

_____

_____(Continue on pages 72-74, if needed.)

Write down the areas of your life that were your outward forms of cover up.

_____

_____

_____

_____

_____

_____

_____

_____

_____

_____

_____(Continue on pages 72-74, if needed.)

UNHEALTHY HABIT PATTERNS—A LIFE OF INDEPENDENCE

Now, as we enter our late teens and early adulthood we are off on a lifelong search for ways of gaining love, acceptance, and security—without realizing it. Out of this search develops unhealthy habit patterns and unrealistic, poor self-images.

Let me give you an example of the two most common unhealthy habit patterns that seem to develop. The first is a **life of independence**. This develops after many years of looking to authority figures for love, acceptance, and security and getting rejected and hurt.

As we are hurt over and over by authority figures, we tend to cut them off until we alone are left as the ultimate, regulating, and controlling factor of our life. Then we go to church and sing songs like "I Surrender All", when in reality we alone hold the controls to our life and are not willing to surrender them even to the Lord. Thus, people are living far more independent lives than they might ever imagine. It is very hard to ask God for His will and guidance for your life while at the same time holding the controls of your life in the palm of your hand.

If you decide to pray about breaking this rejection cycle, this is one of the things that must be surrendered to the Lord. The controls have to be given over completely into His hands and His control. Yes, you are actually going to have to reach out and trust an authority figure again, but in this case the authority is God and He is, and always has been, completely worthy of our trust. We are not to try and live independently of Him; but rather, live completely dependent upon Him.

Write down the areas of your life where you see the stronghold of independence and control. You may as well be honest!

_____

_____

_____

_____

_____

_____(Continue on pages 72-74, if needed.)

UNHEALTHY HABIT PATTERNS—A FEAR OF COMMITMENT

The second unhealthy habit pattern that develops out of this rejection cycle is a **fear of commitment**. As a person receives hurts from various relationships, commitment tends to become harder and harder. Why? It's because we are afraid of being hurt and rejected. Therefore, commitment of any true depth and substance becomes a very real problem for us.

Remember, people are not consciously recognizing what is really going on. How most people handle fear of commitment is simply to limit the number of truly close, committed relationships they have. Thus, most people have one or maybe two really close, committed, open, and vulnerable relationships in their lives. In our minds it boils down to simple math and logic. If I am going to be hurt, then it is better to be hurt by one or two rather than eight or nine.

So we spend our life trying to protect ourselves from relational hurt. We have not realized that all our protection methods are in vain because they are based on the very fear of being rejected. Therefore, we aren't really as free as we think, but rather a slave to the very fear from which we are trying to protect ourselves.

Obviously, this becomes a real problem in areas like marriage contributing to the fifty percent divorce rate. It is also a problem in the area of serving the Lord. People tend to be "committed" to Him only to the unconscious degree that they are still in control.

Again, if you decide to pray about breaking this rejection cycle in your life, this is another specific area that needs to be addressed before the Lord. It is very difficult to ask the Lord for His will and destiny for your life, while at the same time, unconsciously struggling with fear of commitment. This can be one reason why so many prayers seem to go unanswered. Also, this is why so many pastors' visions from God for their congregations go unfulfilled. They are trying to convince people to "get committed" without realizing how truly afraid of commitment the people are.

Write down the areas of your life where the fear of commitment is a real struggle.

_____

_____

_____

_____

_____

_____

_____

_____

_____

_____

_____

_____

_____

_____

_____

_____

_____

_____

_____

_____(Continue on pages 72-74, if needed.)

THE POWER OF THOUGHTS

Now I would like to share a few verses with you. In II Corinthians 10:4-5, it says, *"For the weapons of our warfare are not physical, but they are powerful with God's help for the tearing down of fortresses, inasmuch as we tear down reasonings and every proud barrier that is raised up against the knowledge of God and lead every thought into subjection to Christ."*

In these verses we see that "thoughts" are being compared to fortresses, reasonings, and proud barriers, which are raised up against God's thoughts. As a person walks through this rejection cycle, one of the real bondages that develops is the thoughts that he or she begins to think about himself or herself. These thoughts are not to be taken lightly, but rather as the Bible says, they are fortresses, reasonings, and proud barriers. Do you realize that one thought can literally hold you captive for a lifetime, until the truth is embraced and sets you free?

The fact is, people need freedom from the thoughts they have concluded about themselves. They need to realize where these thoughts have come from and how they have held them captive for much of their lives.

What I would like for you to do is write down the thoughts you have believed about yourself. Let me give you some examples of what people have said about themselves in our seminars:

> I am not smart.
> I am not attractive.
> I have no talents.
> I am just inferior.
> God can't really use me.
> People don't really like me.
> I am just a failure.

WALLS OF BONDAGE

These are the walls of your cage. Just one of these thoughts can hold you in bondage until it is broken by the truth. Believing any of these thoughts has been a major contributor in the forming of a false identity, low self-worth, and low self-esteem.

Let me ask you a question. Where did these thoughts come from? There are really only three sources: you, others, or the devil. There is just one problem with any of these sources; none of them is a true source. Most of the time we are the ones that unconsciously deduced our own lying thought conclusion. Then we spend the rest of our lives believing that lie and living it out as "proof".

Now, I want you to think about this question. Has God ever said any of these things to you? I can tell you right now the answer is "no". God has never said any of these thoughts to us, and yet we have received them into our spirit and soul and lived them out for years.

Not only have we hurt ourselves, by believing these lies, we have also hurt our heavenly Father and very possibly anyone else who is part of our relational life: mom, dad, children, friends.

Here is the good news. It is the truth that sets us free. Do you realize that believing these lies has even kept you from hearing what your heavenly Father has to say to you? I think it is time to pray.

Notes_____

_____

_____

_____

_____

_____

_____

PRAYING INTO THREE AREAS

We are going to pray into three areas.

(1) The first area is this list. What I would like for you to do is write down any wrong thoughts you have believed about yourself.

Wrong thoughts or lies I have believed about myself.

1. _____

_____

2._____

_____

3._____

_____

4._____

_____

5._____

_____

6._____

_____

7._____

_____

Now, let's ask God to forgive you for believing these lies. Then you need to ask the Lord to open your ears to hear what He has always desired to say to you. Understand, you are His child through the blood of Jesus Christ. You are very special to Him. He loves you with all His heart. In spite of everything, He is proud of you and loves you simply because you are His, not for what you may or may not have done. Let these truths sink into the depths of your spirit and begin to walk believing the truth. It may take some time for your emotions to catch up with what you have done in prayer, but don't let that discourage you. That is normal. Walk in the light and the truth, as He is in the light and you will never be the same.

(2)   The second area we need to pray into is the area of a life of independence. Spend time before the Lord and give Him the controls of your life. Put your trust back in Him and trust His control completely.

Pray it through. When I say "pray it through" I mean don't rush. Stay in prayer or keep coming back until you know you have broken through, even if it takes days or weeks.

(3)   The last area to pray into is fear of commitment. Take time praying through the different friendships and relationships you have had. Let the Lord show you how you have built up your own protection and defense system and then give it to Him. Let Him and His love for you become your protection system from now on and forevermore. Pray it through.

We have covered a lot of ground in this teaching. I hope you now have a better understanding of how, even as a Christian, our identity, self-worth, and self-esteem has been so far removed from where God intended it to be. The good news is: as we pray through each of these areas, He is able to restore us. He is able to help us understand and discover our true identity. He is able to help us walk in a freedom we have never known, but which He has always intended for us.

My prayer for you is that as you lay your head down to sleep tonight, may your ears now be open to hear your heavenly Father share with you the things He has always thought about you and desired to tell you. May you be greatly encouraged.

Again, feel free to write and/or doodle on these pages as you continue your soul searching and listening to the Lord.

CHAPTER THREE:
THE PERFORMANCE CYCLE

Chapter Three

TWO QUESTIONS

Unfortunately most of us have had to work, perform, connive, and strive to gain some form of acceptance from others. This leads us to ask two questions.

1. How much of my life is being lived out to win or gain the love and acceptance of others?

2. How much of my life is being lived out to win or gain God's love and acceptance?

DESIRE FOR LOVE AND ACCEPTANCE

Consciously or unconsciously we are after a main ingredient of love called acceptance. Where does this desire for acceptance come from? Basically, as we have explained in our previous studies, God created us for an everlasting love relationship. You cannot have relationship without acceptance. There are many areas in which we strive for acceptance. Obviously, God is one, but this struggle also takes place in desiring acceptance from others, self, the devil, animals—the list is endless. I would like to focus on our desire for acceptance from others.

In I Thessalonians 2:3-6 it says, *"For we never indulged in flattery, as you well know, neither did we use a pretext to satisfy our greed to which God is witness, neither did we seek the acceptance of men, either from you or from others, though as Christ's apostles we were in position to claim authority."* The problem of striving for the acceptance of man has been around a long time. Let me try and explain it like this. We all have a desire to be loved and accepted. This desire came from God. In creating us, God birthed in us a need to be loved and accepted.

The problem is man or other creatures were never meant to be the fulfillment of this God-given desire. God not only gave us the desire to be loved and accepted, but He actually meant for us to look to Him for the fulfillment of these desires. Unfortunately, we spend most of our lives looking everywhere else but to God for fulfillment in these areas. The truth is, only God can truly bring the fulfillment to our desire for love and acceptance.

ACCEPTANCE PRINCIPLE

Let me explain how this works. As we reach out to others for their love and acceptance at any point during our life, without realizing it, we allow them to mold our identity by what they will accept in us. Think it through. If I want to be accepted by the athletic community, what have I got to become like? An athlete. If I want to be accepted by a punk rock group, what have I got to become? I have to dress, act, think, and behave like a punk rock person in every way. You can apply this truth to any gang, group, mom, dad, boyfriend, girlfriend; it will still come out the same.

This is a very powerful principle. So much so, that we need to take a few minutes and look back over our lives. I would like you to write down the significant groups of people or individuals to whom you have reached out for their love and acceptance during your lifetime.

_____

_____

_____

_____

_____

_____

_____

Now I would like for you to write down every single emotion, thought, and character trait that you believe developed as a result of reaching out to these various persons or groups.

_____

_____

_____

_____

_____

_____

_____

_____

I hope you are fully realizing now how powerful this principle really is. How much of your character and personality have been formed by you allowing "others" to dictate what they will accept in you.

Now, here is the good news. It is not too late. Your situation is redeemable. Nothing is too hard for God, including working with you. All you have to do is begin to truly reach out to God for His love and acceptance and guess what, the same principle applies. Yes, your character and personality will be formed by what God will accept in you. But that is okay because that is the way God meant for it to be. As we do this, we will become like Him. We will be taking on the character of Christ and allowing God to truly live and be shown through our life. The consequences of living out a life of looking to others instead of God for love and acceptance produces what I call a performance cycle. Let me walk you through it.

Let's begin with childhood. A child learns to gain love and acceptance through performance. We are not saying this is always wrong, obviously, but I want you to grasp the overall picture. Usually a child is given love and acceptance after he or she does something good, thus learning to perform. My question is this; does

God give us love and acceptance only when we perform correctly for it? No, His love and acceptance are unconditional. I remember when our daughter was very young and I wanted to somehow get this through to her. I would purposefully wait until she was just sitting on the floor doing nothing, then I would come to her and say, "Daddy loves you" so she could not relate it to anything she had done. I could see she loved being told she was loved but was trying to figure out what she had done to deserve it.

FEAR OF FAILURE IN TEENS

Next we move into teen-age years. Many teens, even unknowingly, will develop a fear of failure. Why? What is it they are seeking? Acceptance. What is the biggest threat to their getting acceptance? Failure. Thus, for many teens fear of failure becomes a very real emotional problem. What is sad is that the teens basically have no idea what is going on or why. They just continue to let the fear of failure dominate their lives, sometimes with devastating results, as we have seen in many high school attack situations. I see this scenario in all cultures, but the Asian cultures really bring it to light.

Let's say we are in Japan and a teen is transitioning from high school to the university. He or she has to take university entrance exams. Let's say he or she fails those exams. The feeling of failure is enormous. Because of the extended family cultural concept, he or she has not only failed the entrance exam, he or she has also failed mom, dad, brothers, sisters, aunts, uncles, school friends, neighborhood friends, and dead ancestors. You get the picture. The enormity of this failure has produced in Japan the number one suicide rate in the world for people between ages 18-25. How very sad.

The fear of failure and desire for acceptance are very powerful emotional motivators. If we could only point our hearts toward God and relate firstly to Him, emotional stability and maturity would be ours.

Would you take a few minutes and write down any specific situations in your life where you believe fear of failure played a real part in your thoughts, reactions, emotions or decisions?

_____

_____

_____

_____

_____

_____

_____

_____

_____

_____

_____

_____

_____

_____

_____

_____

_____

_____

_____

_____(Continue on pages 88-90, if needed.)

FEAR OF FAILURE IN ADULTS

The cycle doesn't end here. Now we move from teens into young adulthood. The fear of failure is still motivating our being even though we don't know it. Even unconsciously we will think of ways to protect ourselves against failure as we enter the university and the work world. So the question becomes, how can I protect myself against failure? The answer is very simple, perfectionism or success. So our personality begins to take on these attributes of perfectionism: the belief that we can't afford to make a mistake; the strong sense of competition; and basically no patience with those who don't live up to this standard. Does this sound familiar? This is not a pretty way to grow up. Thus, we see the overwhelming amount of pills taken by this generation is to help control their emotions.

As you look back over your life, write down relationships, situations, and choices you now see as helping you develop perfectionistic tendencies.

_____

_____

_____

_____

_____

_____

_____

_____

_____

_____

_____

_____(Continue on pages 88-90, if needed.)

PRESSURE SITUATIONS

The next step in this cycle is what I call, difficulty with fixed time, or pressure situations. For example, let's say a leader or authority figure approaches you and asks you to do something for him or her within a certain time period. When individuals are struggling in this performance cycle, being asked to do a task or tasks within a designated time frame can seem like being put in a pressure box. Usually the individual's first thought is how can I get out of this box without failing?

Basically, there are only two ways out. For the vast majority of people, the way out of these potential pressure boxes is to work like crazy. In other words they will "work" the assignment through to a place of "perfection" which means they hopefully cannot be accused of failing. Of course, this work-like-crazy philosophy is not based on good old responsible behavior; it is based on fear of failure. The fear is when someone is consciously or unconsciously looking to a leader or authority figure for love and acceptance, the individual will do about anything to keep from failing in the eyes of that authority figure.

There are some individuals who sometimes respond to a fixed time pressure difficulty in a different way. Although "creative" might not be the best word, maybe "sneaky" would be better, these individuals simply come down with temporary sicknesses. This does seem to get them out of the box for the moment but sooner or later they will have to face it again and then the response is usually work-like-crazy. Or they may develop a failure mentality and just accept the fact that sooner or later they are going to get fired, so what difference does it really make? That becomes their excuse for never succeeding.

Can you remember and describe situations where you have felt trapped in a box by a leader or authority figure? How did you handle the situation?

_____

_____

_____

_____

_____

_____

_____

_____

_____

_____

_____

_____

_____(Continue on pages 88-90, if needed.)

SERVING

The next step in our performance cycle has to do with the subject of serving. Usually serving is thought of as a good thing, and rightfully so, however in this example, serving is used as a selfish means to a selfish end. When serving is good, it is done out of a pure heart, with a pure motive, not really looking for or expecting anything in return. In our performance cycle, individuals get caught up in serving in order to get the love and acceptance they so desperately long for and can't seem to get any other way.

Thus, these individuals will consistently volunteer for assignments but, let me make it very clear, if they do not get the accompanying recognition for what they have done, sooner or later, they will react. They will explode, accuse, or simply withdraw into themselves and feed themselves the love and acceptance others failed to give them. You can always tell if someone is serving out of a pure or an impure motive. Just wait for the response or reaction if acknowledgement is not given.

Since we are being open and honest in order to be healed, describe the situations where you realize your motive for serving was not pure but was to gain a form of love and acceptance. Understand, this can happen in the workplace, in church, between husband and wife, or parent and child.

_____
_____
_____
_____
_____
_____
_____
_____
_____
_____
_____
_____
_____

_____(Continue on pages 88-90, if needed.)

PERIODIC WITHDRAWALS

This brings us to the last step in our performance cycles, which are periodic withdrawals. In all of our examples, it is common and probable that sooner or later the individuals will choose forms of withdrawal. But understand clearly what is happening. The withdrawals are for one main purpose: to feed themselves forms of love and acceptance they do not seem to be able to get any other way. Here individuals can be very creative and also very destructive. Drugs, alcohol, pornography, elicit sex, overeating, and over-exercising can all be very destructive forms of feeding ourselves love and acceptance. There are times when individuals may temporarily withdraw to things like the computer, games, movies, books, etc, which may not be as destructive, but the motive for going there is the same.

Now here is what I would like for you to do. Identify the areas you have withdrawn or even still do withdraw to feed yourself false forms of love and acceptance.

_____

_____

_____

_____

_____

_____

_____

_____

_____

_____

_____

_____

_____

_____

_____

_____

_____

_____(Continue on pages 88-90, if needed.)

Obviously, everything you have been writing down is an opportunity for prayer and healing. But just wait a moment as I am going to give you some specifics at the end of the book to hold onto in prayer and in walking into a place of wholeness and healing.

THE REAL PROBLEM

Strange as it may sound, performance is not the problem. Jesus was a tremendous performer but here is the difference. He never performed to get love and acceptance. He was a tremendous performer because He had His Father's love and acceptance and knew it. Gee, isn't this supposed to be the same for the Christian? Christians should be the greatest performers on the face of the earth but sadly, the lack of knowing and walking in the security of Father's love keeps so many from doing what the Lord has called them to do.

The real problem is most people have not realized God's unconditional love and acceptance from their parents, which basically means that the parents never realized God's love and acceptance either. It is very difficult to give what you do not have or know. This is why so many people are hurting emotionally. This is not an excuse but a reality with which one must deal. How do we deal with it? Somebody has got to lay hold of truth and break the cycle for himself or herself and then for succeeding generations.

We can say to our child, "You know, Sweetheart, we love you, but we are only human. We make mistakes. Your heart is crying out deeply for love and acceptance. We can only fulfill that to a certain degree, but God can fulfill it to the nth degree. We want to point you to the loving God who can completely fill your heart's cry. This is what your heart beats for." We can share this hope with our daughters and sons. If we have broken the cycle in our own lives then we can help our children break it in theirs.

Write what the Lord wants you to say to your child:

_____

_____

_____

_____

_____

_____

_____

Chapter Three

How God Brought All This To My Attention

MY PERSONAL EXPERIENCE

I would like to open up my life a bit to you and share how God brought all this to my attention and the choices I had to make to actually apply God's love and acceptance to my emotional being.

I would like to share with you three stories that God used to expose these insecurities in my life. They may not be the most heart wrenching stories you have ever heard. That isn't the point. It was God's way of exposing these cycles in my life and proving His faithfulness to answer my cry for understanding and freedom. Another purpose for the stories is that you may be able to plug in your own story as well and see very clearly what it is going to take for you to walk out of these life cycles into a place of true freedom and security.

FIRST STORY

I had been in missions for only a couple of years and had returned home for a brief break. I had not yet begun to speak nor did I have any idea that the Lord would eventually lead me that way. A church asked if I would do a seminar for them. It was the very first time I had been asked to do a seminar at a church and I was feeling a lot of pressure and stress over it. The Sunday before I was to do the seminar, I was asked to speak in Sunday school at my home church. I spoke and I thought everything went very well. But apparently one person did not appreciate what I had to say and unknown to me went to the pastor and said I was speaking very radical things. The pastor apparently believed her without question. The next thing I knew I got a phone call from my pastor asking me to come in to his office. I was thrilled because I was in these cycles, but didn't know it, and was looking to my pastor for love and acceptance.

I got to his office and basically, he said he understood that I had taught some very radical principles and that I must never do that again. He never asked for my input. Then he asked me to promise to never speak about anything that could possibly cross our denominational lines. I didn't even know I had crossed any lines. I had prayed, asked God what He wanted me to share and gave it. I explained this to him and said I could never agree to what he was asking as I didn't believe I had done anything wrong. His response was to never let me speak again in the church. Neither could I stand up and share to let the people know when I was going back to the mission field. Finally, he said he felt it his duty to call the pastor of the church where I was going to do my very first seminar and advise him not to have me speak.

To say the least, I was devastated. I had come looking for love and acceptance and had gotten blown out of the water. I remember going back to the room where I was staying and feeling so hurt. I knew I had to forgive my pastor and so I did, but the hurt was intense. I asked God a question, unfortunately not the right one as we will see later. I asked what I had done wrong. I didn't feel the Lord convict me of anything, so I figured everything was okay. But it wasn't. There was a deep wound in my spirit and I didn't even know it. I thought since the Lord didn't convict me of anything, everything was just fine.

SECOND STORY

The second story begins a few years later when I was on the mission field working with my leader to develop the counseling ministry for Youth With A Mission. A business person flew over to meet with us and asked if one of the staff could come and minister to their staff for a couple of weeks. I was asked to go and happily accepted. I was flown to this person's business, and I poured all I knew into them over a two week period. (We won't go into the problems this business had and, let me say, the staff members were extremely grateful for what I accomplished there.) I was getting ready to leave when the business owner asked me into the office. Once again, I was looking forward to hearing good things and being appreciated, but no, that wasn't to be.

The scene began with the business owner saying how disappointed they were, though never giving any specifics. It quickly escalated to my being told I needed to pay the company back for the round trip ticket. Again, I was blind-sided. I had truly given all I had and knew God had allowed me to make a difference in the lives of the staff. I found myself beginning to cry uncontrollably, which had never happened before. It took me quite awhile before I gained some composure. I quietly dismissed myself and left. When I got back to where I was staying, I basically did the same thing I did the last time. I prayed and forgave the person and began to ask God what I had done wrong. As before there was no conviction, so I thought everything was fine and taken care of. What I didn't realize was that the wound had only grown larger now, which meant even more insecurity. Asking the Lord who was right and wrong just wasn't the best question, as we will see.

THIRD STORY

This last story takes place a few years later. I was still working with my leader developing the counseling ministry. By now we had a full staff, operating two counseling clinics in the community, running a Biblical Counseling Training School, and a few other things. Needless to say, things were very busy. My leader was and still is a precious man of God, very gentle and caring, but not very good at delegation. When he wasn't there, people would look to me. I was the first one to come along side him from the beginning, but he had never officially given me the title of his assistant. One day he came into a staff meeting and said he was going to give everyone positions of authority. I was so happy to finally get my just reward.

Well, after a few minutes went by, my leader had given everything away to every single person there but me. There was nothing left so I figured I was going to be put over everything as his assistant. He called my name and said, "Steve, I am putting you in charge of marriage seminars." Now that may sound just fine to you, but you need to realize that there was no such animal. We did not have any ministry called family seminars. Basically, my leader had just put me in charge of nothing. If that wasn't bad enough, he began to spiritualize it by saying how we had to birth this new baby. My thought was, *Yea, it's so new it doesn't even exist. You have just put me in charge of nothing after all these years.*

What my leader had done was hit my wound very hard without even realizing it, and boy, did I react. I didn't laugh; I didn't smile; I just prayed and asked the Lord to please end the meeting so I could leave. As I left the meeting, I determined in my heart that I would never trust my leader again. I was hurting more than I knew. Three days passed and the pain never let up. I was avoiding my leader and had no intention of even speaking to him. Then one night at a community meeting, my leader came and stood right beside me. He asked me if everything was all right. Of course I said everything was fine and turned to walk away.

It was in that moment I heard the Lord speak to me very clearly. He said if I did not reach out and begin to trust again, He would take me no further in ministry. In spite of hearing this, I walked away, but the Lord had my attention. I went to my room and began to pray, but this time I asked a different question. Instead of asking who was right or wrong and feeling justified if I had done no wrong, I asked the Lord why was I hurting so much. I could have given obvious answers and justifications for my hurt but this went deeper. This hurt was not normal and I was finally beginning to recognize it and wanted to know why. That question threw me into a most intense time of spiritual warfare. I don't think it lasted very long but it was very intense. Actually, for a while, I thought I was going to die. For some reason that question had opened the way for the Lord to go to the root of the woundedness in my life. The battle had begun to break down all my walls and defenses that I didn't even know were there.

I am not trying to paint an unrealistic picture here, but I want you to understand that to break out of some of the messes in which we find ourselves, it may become a bit intense. It may require us to press into God and not let go until understanding and breakthrough come. [Unfortunately, in this day and age, Christians aren't taught to do much pressing into God at all. They just want everything handed to them and if they have to actually press in and battle in spiritual warfare, forget it. They will just revert to intellectual justification and keep right on in the way they were going.] In the midst of this very intense time, the Lord spoke and said I had been relating to my leader as a father figure. I told the Lord I didn't understand that because I didn't hate my dad. Then the Lord said it wasn't because I hated him but because my dad was just never around and I had longed for his love and acceptance ever since I was a child. All I had done throughout my life was transfer this longing from one authority figure to another. When the Lord said this, it broke me and I began to cry and cry and cry. Then the Lord said I could never go back and get my dad's love and acceptance, but that if I would look to Him to meet these emotional needs, He would fulfill them.

What a simple but profound revelation. How many Christians come to God for salvation but never truly look to Him to meet the deep emotional needs of their lives. Thus, they spend their whole lives looking to things or people for what only God can truly meet. I began to pray for my dad. I forgave him, my mom, and anybody else I could think of. I began to feel so different. I was also truly looking to God for my love and acceptance and He was giving it. I felt so good. I asked the Lord if there was anything else He would like for me to do. The Lord took me up on that and, to my amazement, He asked if I would take a married couple out and buy them a snack (which was all I could afford). This may sound as strange to you as it did to me until I asked the Lord why. He said it is because you have become very selfish and you need to learn how to give to others. That was quite embarrassing, but quite true, so I did exactly what the Lord asked.

This is a very important principle here. As you are asking God for what He would have you do to break out of your cycles, it is important to do exactly what He asks, silly as it may sound. It may be significant and even difficult for you to do. It was difficult for me, but I did it and something broke in me. I began to feel freer than I ever had in my life. Well this encouraged me to ask the Lord again if there was anything else He would have me do. To my amazement the Lord said there was one other thing and of course, I said, "Anything Lord." Then the Lord said something that put me in one of those boxes with seemingly no way out. He asked me to tell others who I really was. Don't misunderstand here: there was no secret life, He was talking about the selfishness. I knew what I had to do, but I didn't want to do it. How many of you would like to stand up in front of your peers and tell them your flaws? I could not find any way out of the box in which the Lord had put me except to do it.

So at the first staff meeting the conviction came, and I knew I had to share. I stood up and began to shake and sweat. I could hardly speak but out it came. I told them they needed to know I was a selfish person, that I didn't really love them, had very little compassion for others, and wanted to ask their forgiveness. I will tell you, something in me broke. Although I thought I was going to die, I didn't, but something inside me did. I had never felt so free in all my life. I went back to the Lord and asked if there was anything else He would have me do, and again to my amazement He said, "No, nothing new. I just want you to do that again to a different group." I remember telling the Lord I almost died the first time but I would do it. So sure enough, another time with another group, I stood up and did it all again with the shaking and the whole works, but I got through it. I felt so free. This was incredible to me, so I asked the Lord if there was anything else. He said to do it one more time and I did.

I have never been the same since. I went back to my leader and shared with him the whole story and we began the family counseling ministry. We have been very close friends ever since—for over thirty years now. You see, the work God did actually freed me up to give myself to my leader without looking for or expecting anything from him in return. I was now getting such amazing love and acceptance emotionally from God. It was wonderful.

Now, anything worth its salt is going to be tested and some very severe tests came. I will tell you right now, you will be tested because the enemy would love to see you revert again to you becoming your own protection from hurts and wounds. But if you will pass the tests, you truly will never be the same. Hopefully you will break these cycles, not only for yourself but also for your family, children and others.

And so there have been tests. I will share just one with you. It wasn't long after all this happened. I was speaking somewhere and during a break while talking on the phone to an old friend, we began joking about some of our experiences in YWAM. It was all in fun, nothing critical or derogatory at all. However, I didn't realize it, but one of the main leaders overheard my side of the conversation and mistook it for a criticism of YWAM. The next thing I know, I was being asked to meet this leader in his office. Again, I was so happy, looking forward to this opportunity, and yes, you guessed what happened. It was pretty much the same scenario of "how could you?" with no room for explanation. I crawled out of there feeling all the old emotions come on me again.

It was at that moment the Lord spoke and asked me what I was going to do. I realized very clearly for the first time that this was a test. I had a choice to defeat the enemy or to go back to building walls of protection around myself. I stopped right there and prayed forgiveness toward this leader and told the Lord I never ever wanted to build another wall of self-protection. I confessed that God's love and acceptance were sufficient for me. I knew then how much this walk of freedom was to be a walk of complete vulnerability, trusting fully in the sufficiency of God's love and acceptance for me, emotionally and in every other way.

Here is what I would ask you to do. Follow these specific instructions I said I was going to give you about praying and walking into a place of wholeness and healing. (See p. 86.) Go to the Lord and ask Him why you are still hurting so much. Allow Him to expose whatever He feels is necessary for your healing. (Write His answers on the next page.) Pray through whatever the Lord shows you, extending forgiveness and whatever else is necessary. Then ask the Lord if there is anything else He would have you do to walk out your healing. The Lord won't give you a list of a hundred things, but He will ask you to do a few very specific things. Those are the things you must do in complete obedience, even while everything in you is yelling that you can't do it. As you walk out what God asks, in obedience, you will taste freedom like never before. Walking out what God asks brings you into His love, acceptance, and security for you. May you forevermore stay there.

In His Love,
Dr. Steve Shamblin

What is the Lord saying about why you are still hurting?

_____
_____
_____
_____
_____
_____
_____
_____
_____
_____
_____
_____
_____
_____
_____
_____

Who is the Lord saying you need to forgive?

_____
_____
_____
_____

What specific things is the Lord telling you to do for your healing? Describe your walk of obedince to Lord and how it has set you free.

_____

_____

_____

_____

_____

_____

_____

_____

_____

_____

_____

_____

_____

_____

_____

_____

_____

_____

_____

_____

_____

_____

Continue to write down how you are feeling and how the healing is being manifest in your life as time goes by.

_____

_____

_____

_____

_____

_____

_____

_____

_____

_____

_____

_____

_____

_____

_____

_____

_____

TO SCHEDULE DR. SHAMBLIN:

FOR A SPEAKING ENGAGEMENT
OR TO GIVE A SEMINAR:

steveshamblin@me.com

FOR PERSONAL COUNSELING (FOR A FEE):
(Dr. Shamblin does counseling for people
around the world, for a fee, via skype.)

skype name: sshamblin

TO SEE MANY OTHER RESOURCES:
(For the first time, Dr. Shamblin now has available
a complete DVD set of this seminar,
Healing of the Fractured Soul.)

goforthministries.com

(Note: goforthministries.org and .net are not Dr. Shamblin's website.)

This Book Is Available At:

olivepresspublisher.org

amazon.com

barnesandnoble.com

etc.

BOOK STORE MANAGERS may obtain this book
at 40% discount and returnable through

Olive Press Publisher

by e-mailing: olivepressbooks@gmail.com

or at a lower discount and returnable through

Ingram Book Company

Hope This Book Blessed You.

(Plans are for Dr. Shamblin's second
book, *Pathways to Maturity*,
to come out later this year.)

CPSIA information can be obtained at www.ICGtesting.com
Printed in the USA
BVOW030756080113

309717BV00005B/10/P